Words of Wellbeing, A to Z

Inspiration for Connecting to Joy and Inner Peace

By Kate Vredevoogd
Illustrated by Miette Bennich

Words of Wellbeing, A to Z
Copyright © 2021 by Kate Vredevoogd, Wanderlust Words Publications

For more about this author please visit www.wanderlustwords.com and for more about this artist please visit @miette_paints on Instagram

All rights reserved. No part of this publication may be reproduced, distributed, or transmitted in any form or by any means, including photocopying, recording, or other electronic or mechanical methods, without the prior written permission of the publisher, except in the case of brief quotations embodied in critical reviews and certain other noncommercial uses permitted by copyright law.

Editing by The Pro Book Editor
Illustrated by Miette Bennich
Interior and Cover Design by IAPS.rocks

Main category—BODY, MIND & SPIRIT / Inspiration & personal growth
Other category—SELF-HELP / Personal growth / Happiness

First Edition

To one of my first and greatest teachers. You are in the stars now, Dad, where your guiding light continues to shine.

Bruce Allen Vredevoogd, 1952-2021.

A — awareness.

"Be clearly aware of the stars and infinity on high. Then life seems almost enchanted after all."
—Vincent Van Gogh

"As soon as you honor the present moment, all unhappiness and struggle dissolve, and life begins to flow with joy and ease. When you act out the present-moment awareness, whatever you do becomes imbued with a sense of quality, care, and love—even the most simple action."
—Eckhart Tolle, *The Power of Now: A Guide to Spiritual Enlightenment*

Reflection:

I once heard a story about a Zen meditation teacher who walked behind his meditating students and hit them on the head. If they received the blow, it meant they were lost in their thoughts and not practicing mindful awareness. The other students, who were completely aware and present, could sense the teacher behind them and moved out of the way. Although this particular teaching method seems unnecessarily brutish, it does illustrate the power of awareness.

Think about the last time you took a shower. Did you feel the warm water run over your skin, or were you thinking about yourself in the past or future? When you listen to people, are you hearing their words and aware of their presence, or are you somewhere else, preparing your response or reliving past situations? Life can be an ongoing meditation if we bring our awareness to the present moment, which is the only moment that is really real. If we can anchor ourselves in our bodies and become aware of our breath, that awareness brightens colors, intensifies smells, sharpens our senses, and gives life the richness that it lacks when we are in our ego. To bring your awareness back to the present moment, notice your fingertips and *feel* your sense of touch. Notice your breath move your abdomen. Imagine your energy flowing back into your body and feel it from the inside. Be where you are and anchor yourself there.

B — breathe.

> "I took a deep breath and listened to the old brag of my heart. I am, I am, I am."
>
> —Sylvia Plath, *The Bell Jar*

Reflection:

Your breath is your oldest and most loyal friend—albeit possibly the most under-appreciated. Let's try something together. Take a deep breath, slowly filling all four corners of your lungs with new, fresh air. Let your belly expand. Feel your lungs stretch. Hold it. Let it out, exhaling more slowly than you inhaled to push out every last bit of stale, stagnant air until your lungs crave another breath. Give your body another breath. Doesn't that feel good?

Any time we give the body what it needs, we feel pleasure. Enjoy the experience of giving your body the breath it desires. Let it become your essence and the reality of your being. Turn to your breath as you turn to an old friend. Let it anchor you in the present moment and comfort you when you're upset. Sink into your breath like you sink into a hug and enjoy its embrace.

C — create.

"Do whatever brings you to life [...]. Follow your own fascinations, obsessions, and compulsions. Trust them. Create whatever causes a revolution in your heart."

"A creative life is an amplified life. It's a bigger life, a happier life, an expanded life, and a hell of a lot more interesting life. Living in this manner—continually and stubbornly bringing forth the jewels that are hidden within you—is a fine art, in and of itself."

—Elizabeth Gilbert, *Big Magic: Creative Living Beyond Fear*

Reflection:

One of my English students has spent his life following instructions to a T. He is a mechanical engineer who only buys black and gray t-shirts, reads strictly nonfiction, and until recently, has believed himself to be incapable of exercising creative expression. While teaching him English over the past two years, I've changed his mind because, as it turns out, speaking a foreign language is an inherently creative activity. You have to find similar vocabulary and parallel expressions and use analogies and metaphors and creative solutions to express yourself. What could be more creative than that?

He comes from the world of mathematics where there is only one correct answer, one clear solution to the problem, and perfection does exist. The world of creativity doesn't offer you that security because you must make decisions that best express what *you* want to say in order to express your creativity. There is room for interpretation, and perfection doesn't exist. This world empowers us to read between lines, find hidden meanings, and know that there is no wrong or right answer.

We are all creative beings, and our creativity can be accessed at any point. Nobody is excluded from creativity. Some people are more tapped into it than others, and some manifest their creativity in more standard ways, such as painting, writing, and playing music. All humans are creative, but like my English student, some may not realize it. Gardening is creative. So is baking, building, doing origami, and rearranging furniture.

When you feel disconnected from your creativity, think back to what you did when you were ten years old. What did you do then? Did you paint model soldiers? Did you cut paper snowflakes? Did you make beautiful cakes with your easy-bake oven? Did you draw cartoons or braid your sister's hair? Whatever it is, do that! Let your inner child guide you back to your creative impulses.

D — dream.

> "Hold fast to dreams,
> For if dreams die,
> Life is a broken-winged bird
> That cannot fly."
> —Langston Hughes

> "Consciousness succumbs all too easily to unconscious influences, and these are often truer and wiser than our conscious thinking."
> —Carl Jung

Reflection:

I can't imagine my life without dreams, and I don't mean the hopes and dreams kind. I mean those wild fantasy movies that play in my head every night. But what are they? Descartes thought dreams were a waste of time, which makes sense from a rationalist perspective since neuroscience has discovered that the prefrontal cortex—or the logic and critical thinking center of the brain—takes a biochemical nap during dream time. Freud thought dreams were repressed—usually sexual—desires being expressed by the id, otherwise known as the unconscious mind. Jung focused more on symbols and imagery, believing that dreams were a bridge between the unconscious and conscious mind, communicating clues to solving problems occupying our conscious mind.

Some people believe dreams are images from past lives or communication from beings on other energetic planes. Others assert that they are simply aleatory compositions of sounds and images thrown together by the brain while it resets every night. I think dreams are a sort of dialogue with ourselves and all the things we perceive and intuit, occasionally with a collective consciousness. I tend to agree with Jung in his assertion that dreams hold wisdom and insight into the things that trouble us during our waking hours. Try keeping a dream journal or record a voice memo in the mornings to remember your dreams. There may be patterns or symbols that can unlock that creative block. This may shine a light on a possible solution to a problem that your conscious mind has been unable to resolve.

E — explore.

"Nobody ever figures out what life is all about, and it doesn't matter. Explore the world. Nearly everything is really interesting if you go into it deeply enough."

—Richard P. Feynman

Reflection:

You don't need extravagant travel plans to explore and engage in the world around you. Traveling isn't always an option for everyone, which we learned collectively during 2020. Besides, global restrictions aside, many people's personal finances don't allow for trips to Bali or Peru.

There is much to learn from and enjoy wherever you find yourself in the world. Take a day trip to places like the mountains, a small town you've never been to, a museum in your city that you've never visited, an orchard or a vineyard, or a wildlife reserve. Keep your eyes and minds open and explore.

I would also encourage you not to limit your exploration to the physical plane. After all, the idea behind Wanderlust Words is to take the concept of wanderlust, which is that urge to explore uncharted territories, and turn it inward. This will channel that longing for stimulation and revelatory new experiences, using it to explore the depths of your being and excavating your soul for the diamonds that lie within. You can mirror your physical journey into the unknown with a metaphorical journey into your consciousness, where the exploration is limitless.

F — friendship.

" 'Why did you do all this for me?' he asked. 'I don't deserve it. I've never done anything for you.'

'You have been my friend,' replied Charlotte. 'That in itself is a tremendous thing.' "

—E.B. White, *Charlotte's Web*

Reflection:

We need community, and we thrive when we feel connected. Having satisfying, mutually loving relationships with other beings is at the heart of wholeness. It's important that we show our appreciation for the other beings in our lives through support, non-judgement, and just being there. Our friendships change and evolve as we do, which is normal and natural, but friendships can also fade away if we don't actively take care of them. Things like a phone call, a birthday card, a thoughtful question, or a lunch-date may seem like small gestures, but they can play a significant role in letting people know that we care and want to stay connected. On the other hand, if someone gives you the gift of friendship, don't take it for granted. A true friend doesn't give to receive, they give because they love, but when love is reciprocal, it blooms and becomes the most precious treasure.

G — gratitude.

> "The root of joy is gratefulness...It is not joy that makes us grateful; it is gratitude that makes us joyful."
>
> —David Steindl-Rast

Reflection:

Brother David Steindl-Rast, a monk and interfaith scholar, speaks prolifically about gratitude. In his exquisite meditations on gratefulness, he postulates that although most of us think that happy people are grateful, the truth is that grateful people are happy. Gratefulness leads us to happiness. He says that gratefulness occurs when we are given something truly valuable that we haven't worked for, bought, or earned. When we receive this gift, gratitude fills our hearts, and when this happens, happiness fills our hearts as well.

If we can learn to live gratefully instead of having occasional grateful experiences, we can live joyfully. All we need to do is open our awareness to the many gifts we are being given in every moment of every day. These gifts are not always material. If gratefulness doesn't come to you in a natural way, you can incorporate a gratefulness practice to help you harmonize with your gratitude. Mealtimes can be a great opportunity to speak about what you were given that day. I've used gratitude boxes in my classrooms as well as at home, which also allows for the super feel-good tradition of reading through the notes of gratitude at the end of the week. You could also begin your journal entries with something you're grateful for.

H — honesty.

"If you do not tell the truth about yourself you cannot tell it about other people."
—Virginia Woolf

Reflection:

Being honest with ourselves is not only more difficult than being honest with others, but it is also a prerequisite. If I don't know that I'm scared, that my boundaries are being crossed, or that my needs aren't being met, how can I communicate it to other people? Being honest with yourself takes courage because the truth is often much more uncomfortable than the lies we tell ourselves—that's why we tell them.

Meditation can connect you to your truth. Journaling and time alone, walks in nature, and unhurried pauses have helped me see through the clouds and identify what's real in my heart. When we connect with our truth, the fog around us lifts, and other truths become more visible as well. When you can cut through the tricks, justifications, and excuses and see yourself for who you really are, you will be able to do the same with others.

1 — inward.

> "What we seek, at the deepest level, is inwardly to resemble, rather than physically to possess, the objects and places that touch us through their beauty."
>
> —Alain de Botton, *The Architecture of Happiness*

Reflection:

The belief that acquisition of material goods can increase our inner value and beauty is one of the great perpetuators of human suffering, and it is the furthest thing from the truth. If it were true, depression and insecurity would only afflict the less affluent, and those with unlimited access to material things would be the pinnacle of contentment and high self-worth. We are told from an early age that money can't buy happiness, yet no matter where we look in Western capitalist society, we find what we are lacking and then consume a product or experience to fill that void. But nothing external can ever fill a spiritual void. Ever. Instead of trying to possess things, we should let the material things in this world reach us on a spiritual level. When something external strikes us as beautiful, we can allow ourselves to be touched by that beauty. We can then allow it to move and alter something inside of ourselves, incorporating it into the fiber of our being.

J—journal.

> "The journal is a vehicle for my sense of selfhood. It represents me as emotionally and spiritually independent. Therefore (alas) it does not simply record my actual, daily life but rather—in many cases—offers an alternative to it."
>
> —Susan Sontag, *Reborn: Journals and Notebooks, 1947-1963*

Reflection:

There are no rules to journaling. Journaling is a conversation with yourself. It's the slowing down of your thoughts and then funneling them into sentences and the occasional illustration. There's no judgment or pressure—which opens up space for honesty and clarity. You don't have to be a writer to keep a journal. You just have to be a human being with thoughts, feelings, and interactions with and reactions to the world.

Amazing things can happen on the pages of a journal, but we can never expect them to because expectations are the antithesis of journaling. Try writing half a page at the beginning or end of the day. If you are new to journaling, start by simply recounting the day's events. As you get more comfortable with your routine, begin to weave in some reflections about your experiences that will lead you down trains of thought. When you finish, close your journal. Journals aren't for reading just after writing them.

K — kindness.

"Be kind whenever possible. It is always possible."
—Dalai Lama XIV

Reflection:

Have you ever asked yourself why it so frequently seems easier to be curt than to be kind? Sometimes, it even feels impossible. First of all, it's important to note that the kindness we show others is a direct reflection of the kindness we give ourselves. When we're balanced, centered, and in harmony within ourselves, reacting with kindness instead of anger becomes more natural. Conversely, when we're suffering internally, our ego will push us to take our suffering out on the people around us. We will try to pull them down with us because, as they say, misery loves company. The truth is that it does take more effort to be kind, especially when we're discontent with the world. But it can be deeply satisfying and even surprising when we find the strength to make it happen. Another common saying encourages us to kill it with kindness, and although it shouldn't be our motivation, our kindness is occasionally rewarded with more kindness in return. If someone is mistreating you, maybe all they need is to be shown how to do it better. Show them through kindness, and perhaps they'll follow your example. And if they don't? By being kind in the first place, you were kind to yourself. You nourished your own moral fiber, and that's where the most important healing takes place.

L — love.

> "The way of the miracle-worker is to see all human behavior as one two things: either love, or a call for love."
>
> —Marianne Williamson

Reflection:

Love is the most important word in any given language, but the many definitions of the word don't do it justice. According to the Cambridge Dictionary of English, love is the feeling of being romantically and sexually attracted to another adult or can also refer to having strong feelings of liking a friend or person in your family. So love is just a more intense liking of something? Um, no.

According to Merriam-Webster, love is a "strong affection for another arising out of kinship or personal ties." This is a better definition, but not great. When translating the Real Academia Española (la RAE) from Spanish, that dictionary calls love "an intense human feeling, coming from one's own insufficiency, which causes the need to look for and find a union with another." What? Love is not a feeling that fills a void, nor an impulse to find a union—love understands that we are all already united.

I'm going to try my hand at defining love: Love is the light that is turned on when you understand that everything is connected, that you don't end where your body ends, that—in the words of Rumi—you are not a drop of water, but the entire ocean in one drop. Love is looking into another person's eyes and seeing yourself.

M — magic.

> "And above all, watch with glittering eyes the whole world around you because the greatest secrets are always hidden in the most unlikely places. Those who don't believe in magic will never find it."
>
> —Roald Dahl

Reflection:

Magic is everywhere, and it is the spark that lights our awe. There's magic in a landscape, a star-filled sky, and a beautiful piece of art. Beyond the usual suspects, there's magic in small, subtle things that we may rarely pause long enough to appreciate. Awe is a feeling of reverence and admiration inspired by something grand or sublime. Awe overcomes me when it starts to rain heavily, as it can do here on the Mediterranean coast, and the fog is so thick that I can barely see my hands if I stretch my arms out in front of me. I feel it when my dear friend sends me videos of her sons seeing or doing something for the first time. Their awe inspires my awe. I feel it when my partner shows me compassion in my ugly moments and hugs me instead of lashing out. I feel it when my dog, Lola, waits for my other, more intrepid dog, Laila, when we're hiking because she doesn't want her to get lost. I feel it when my hibiscus flowers blossom. When do you feel it?

n — nature.

"The clearest way into the Universe is through a forest wilderness."
—John Muir

Reflection:

Jutting gray skyscrapers, city lights, and traffic noise make me want to crawl into myself. I yearn for the soft and still place that I go to when I'm surrounded by nature. Don't get me wrong. Cities are amazing places full of culture and innovation. I love to visit the city, but nothing heals my soul like the sweet stillness of nature.

You know that feeling of calm, serenity, and being grounded after spending a day at the beach, wiggling your bare feet in the sand? Studies have shown numerous health benefits to "grounding"—the practice of placing your bare feet directly on the earth and absorbing the earth's negative electrons through the soles of your feet. It's been shown to reduce inflammation, improve sleep, relieve pain and enhance mood, among many other things. Time spent in the woods or the mountains is like a visit home after spending ages on the road. It settles and anchors me. It's a reminder that most of the things in my life are actually superfluous. Nature teaches us the power of regeneration and the beautiful reality of interconnectedness. Nature is what always was before humans made anything else. Nature is the real OG.

O — observe.

> "The ability to observe without evaluating is the highest form of intelligence."
> —Jiddu Krishnamurti

Reflection:

Observing while reserving judgment allows us to appreciate an event without holding it relative to another. It frees us of comparisons, and when we aren't comparing, we become more grateful and less likely to desire something more. There is so much to learn through observation—even more so when we refrain from evaluating what we've observed—since our evaluations can easily include a logical fallacy or incorrect deduction.

Years ago, I arrived at the grocery store to find mayhem in the parking lot. It was a Friday evening before a three-day weekend, and I had to circle around and around the parking lot before I found a spot. People had been so desperate that they'd fashioned parking spaces where they didn't even exist. When I finally found a space, I had to pull in at an angle, as the two cars on either side had parked outside of their lines. I was so relieved to finally get to my shopping.

As long as I'm not hungry, I actually delight in a trip to the grocery store. I take my time, consider new recipes, try some samples—it's a blast. After an hour of this particular shopping trip, I got back to my car and found a note scribbled and left under my windshield wiper that said, "Nice parking job. Try thinking of other people next time, asshole!" As the sensitive creature that I am, and since I hadn't yet learned the power of not taking things personally, this note broke my heart. The cars around mine had left, and new vehicles had arrived. This time, they parked straight and within their lines, making me look like a jerk who had double-parked to anyone who observed and evaluated.

P — perception.

> "If you are distressed by anything external, the pain is not due to the thing itself, but to your estimate of it; and this you have the power to revoke at any moment."
>
> —Marcus Aurelius, *Meditations*

Reflection:

We are given a choice at every moment. We can choose to hold fast to our perceived reality, with all of its interpretations and judgments, or step back. Everything we perceive passes through a filter, which is different for each person and is formed by our childhood experiences, the agreements we've made with ourselves, the way we identify with our ego, the beliefs we have about our thoughts, and so forth. When our perceptions pass through that filter, we give them an interpretation, and then we give the interpretation a value judgment. It is a mistake to fall into the trap of thinking there is one true reality, and an even bigger mistake is to believe that the interpretations of our perceived reality constitute that one true reality.

The linguistic relativity hypothesis states that the language one speaks affects the way one thinks. In the Russian language, there is no single generic word for the color blue. Instead, a Russian speaker must make an obligatory distinction between lighter blues, "*goluboy*," and darker blues, "*siniy*." A study at MIT offered evidence of cross-linguistic differences in color perception, showing that Russian speakers were actually quicker than English speakers to *perceive* different shades of blue. This was not because their eyes were different, but their language had conditioned them to be more perceptive. If language can affect how we perceive colors, imagine how a single person's collection of experiences could color how they perceive reality.

Q — quiet.

"The quieter you become, the more you can hear."
—Ram Dass

"if

the ocean

can calm itself,

so can you.

we

are both

salt water

mixed with

air."

—Nayyirah Waheed

Reflection:

Blaise Pascal once said, "All of humanity's problems stem from man's inability to sit quietly in a room alone." This famous quote reminds me that restlessness, anxiety, and boredom are not modern-day misfortunes, but they are basic obstacles that form part of the human experience. It is true that now, more than ever, it's easier to distract ourselves and numb our pain using our technological gadgets. Even so, sitting quietly alone has never been easy.

When we are still, we can hear our inner thoughts. Sometimes they're unpleasant, but they also contain insight that can't be accessed without quiet listening. Most of the time, we don't realize when we're dissociating from an uncomfortable emotion or situation, especially when we use technology and external stimulation like watching television. Years ago, I used to have the TV on constantly. I would put a series on my phone to keep me company while I cooked dinner, or I'd leave the news on while cleaning the house, just for some background noise. I didn't realize that I was avoiding being alone with myself, and I definitely didn't realize that the constant noise and stimulation weakened my connection with my intuition and guiding light. I didn't grasp the value of turning everything off, even the lights, and just sitting in quiet darkness. But I do now. When we turn off the lights, we can see the stars. When we turn off the sound, we can hear our hearts.

R — reflect.

"All the advice you ever gave your partner is for you to hear."
—Byron Katie, *Question Your Thinking, Change the World*

Reflection:

Byron Katie's inquiry process, which she calls The Work, is all about reflection. She teaches us to question our thoughts in a way that leads us to a new understanding of a painful situation. With this new understanding, we can find that a lot of the time, our suffering is caused by the thoughts we choose to believe.

Inquiry reflection involves asking yourself four questions about a belief that causes you pain. I'm going to choose the belief: *My partner always has to be right*. The first question to ask yourself is if this belief is true. I would answer that it is. Next, ask yourself if you can absolutely *know* it's true. In this case, I'd have to say no. How can I ever truly know what someone else is feeling or the true motivations behind their actions? Next, ask yourself how you react when you believe the thought. In my case, I feel frustrated. I feel defensive, closed off, and I need him to know that he's wrong. I need him to see that I'm actually right. Now, ask yourself who you would be without the thought. Imagine yourself there. If I didn't believe my partner always needed to be right, I wouldn't need to defend my position. I'd be accepting of his opinion, and I wouldn't need to change it. I'd be satisfied with knowing that I don't need him to agree with me. I'd be open to the possibility that he *is* right. I'd be a better listener. I'd be receptive. The final step is the turnaround, which means that I will flip the thought around and examine each new expression to try it on. Does it hold any truth? My turnaround is that I always need to be right. When I believe that he needs to be right, I defend my position with a white-knuckled grip, and I don't listen. I reject what he says, and I become the person that I believe him to be. If I release this belief, I free myself. This type of reflection can help us question our filters, owning our roles, and the negative and prescriptive thoughts in the conflict. By doing this, we may gain empathy and understanding.

S — synchronicity.

> "According to Vedanta, there are only two symptoms of enlightenment [...]. The first symptom is that you stop worrying. Things don't bother you anymore. You become light-hearted and full of joy. The second symptom is that you encounter more and more meaningful coincidences in your life, more and more synchronicities. And this accelerates to the point where you actually experience the miraculous."
>
> —Deepak Chopra, *Synchrodestiny: Harnessing the Infinite Power of Coincidence to Create Miracles*

Reflection:

In my world view, there are no coincidences and no meaningless events. Everything has meaning, the meaning we give it and the meaning we're open to accepting. Synchronicity is a word used by Carl Jung, which describes "circumstances that appear meaningfully related yet lack a causal connection." Apophenia, on the other hand, was a term coined by Klaus Conrad, a German neurologist and psychiatrist, which refers to the "unmotivated seeing of connections [accompanied by] a specific feeling of abnormal meaningfulness."

What is Deepak Chopra referring to in his book, *Synchrodestiny*? Is it the human tendency to look for patterns where they don't exist, or is it something more? My own experience with synchronicity has been more like a collaboration with the divine. As I awaken spiritually, my intuition becomes stronger and my perception sharpens. I've learned to pick up clues, almost as if this dance on earth were a treasure hunt, leading me to the lessons I need to grow spiritually. I find that synchronicity is being receptive to those clues and following them, trusting the right information will arrive at the right time to help us along our paths to self-evolution. The more present and spiritually connected you become, the more easily you will be able to recognize the loose threads that are meant to be tugged, which will help you unravel the illusion and bring you closer to truth.

T—tolerance.

> "Nothing other people do is because of you. It is because of themselves. All people live in their own dream, in their own mind; they are in a completely different world from the one we live in. When we take something personally, we make the assumption that they know what is in our world, and we try to impose our world on their world."
>
> —Don Miguel Ruiz, *The Four Agreements: A Practical Guide to Personal Freedom*

Reflection:

If we speak of tolerance in terms of social justice, Ayaan Hirsi Ali said it best: "Tolerance of intolerance is cowardice." But tolerance specifically applied to our interpersonal relationships can be explored via the second agreement in the book *The Four Agreements*, which is "Don't take anything personally."

I think the foundation of tolerance, the fertile soil that allows it to grow, is understanding that nothing is about you. Nothing anyone says or does—their reactions or their insults—is actually about you. Remember that in the mirror effect, we reflect our feelings about ourselves onto other people? Keep this in mind the next time someone treats you poorly or criticizes you. That person is reflecting something that they don't tolerate within themselves or don't accept about their own actions. And furthermore, when you take something personally, you're admitting its truth. If you have a deep and true sense of self-worth, it becomes much easier to see when someone's criticisms are valid growth points or just projections of their own insecurities. Recognizing that we all live in different realities can help us be more tolerant of others and avoid holding them to standards that the limitations of their worlds make it impossible for them to reach.

U — unlearn.

"To attain knowledge, add things every day. To attain wisdom, remove things every day."
—Lao Tzu

Reflection:

I used to have a therapist who was very interested in boundary setting and labeling people and relationships as "toxic." She taught me to evaluate my relationships according to what each person offered me and what I received from the relationship. When someone didn't put the same energy into the relationship that I did, she taught me that this person was taking advantage of me, and I needed to set a boundary with that "toxic person." This understanding of give and take led me to form a system of expectations that set me up for a state of constant indignation. Whatever I invested in a relationship became a sort of relationship currency that denoted the value of my love, and when I wasn't paid back with that same love, I felt cheated.

After a series of profound disappointments, I began reflecting. I learned about love languages and how people express their appreciation in different ways. I learned that what people do and how they treat me isn't an indication of my worth, but it is a reflection of how they feel about themselves. Finally, I learned that when I give and expect something in return, I'm putting a condition on my love. I've learned to pay attention to other people's love language until I become fluent in it. I've learned that if someone treats me poorly, it's because they are suffering. I've learned that when I invest energy in a relationship and show compassion to someone I care about, the light inside me grows. I don't need anything back because I'm already receiving.

Boundaries are important, and when we spend an extended amount of time with someone who is in their ego, we may need to set those boundaries and take our space. I had to unlearn everything that I thought I knew about boundaries and toxicity to see beyond my initial understanding, which helped me move out of defensiveness and resentment and into a place of compassion.

V — vulnerability.

"Embracing our vulnerabilities is risky but not nearly as dangerous as giving up on love and belonging and joy—the experiences that make us the most vulnerable. Only when we are brave enough to explore the darkness will we discover the infinite power of our light."

—Brené Brown

Reflection:

When Brené Brown, a self-defined researcher-storyteller, began her investigation about human connection, her research led her to examine shame, courage, worthiness, and vulnerability. Through six years of collecting data, participating in focus groups, and listening to stories, she came to the conclusion that vulnerability was the key to connection and living a life full of joy, creativity, belonging, and love. Her job as a researcher was to control and predict. She discovered that a full and happy life consisted of a "spiritual awakening," a term her therapist told her. This included suppressing the urge to control and predict during the times she felt like she was having a breakdown.

Being vulnerable takes guts. It allows you to be authentic, letting go of who you think you are supposed to be and stepping into who you are. When we allow ourselves to be vulnerable, we also allow ourselves to be loved in a real way. Rather than having a forced, fake or conditional love, we get to experience real, authentic love. Nothing is more satisfying than being seen for who you are and being loved without pretense.

W — willingness.

"Confront the dark parts of yourself, and work to banish them with illumination and forgiveness. Your willingness to wrestle with your demons will cause your angels to sing."

—August Wilson

Reflection:

The possibility for self-development is always there. The resources are available to anyone who has access to the internet or possesses a library card. There are teachers all around us who can guide us if we let them. That being said, taking responsibility for your presence in this world and dedicating the time and energy to making sense of it all—to find order in the chaos—is a daunting journey. Finding and facing the parts of you that cause you shame, and shedding light and love on those parts, is noble and necessary if you want to be a real participant in this collective reality and have any amount of control over your experience on this physical plane. More important than courage, emotional intelligence, having a spiritual background, or having any sort of training whatsoever in the fields of self-development is willingness. If you're willing to confront your darkness, stand face to face with your demons and say, "Okay. Let's talk." Things will align, and the opportunities will present themselves for you to do that work. Just say you're ready, and the work will come.

X — expand.

"Life shrinks or expands in proportion to one's courage."
—Anais Nin

Reflection:

The world is a big and beautiful—and sometimes terrifying—place. When we expect small things from life because that's what we feel we deserve, we receive small things. When we are small, our world is small, but when we grow and expand, the possibilities we're given grow as well.

I have to take this moment to recognize that throughout history, expansion has been encouraged in men and suppressed—to varying and sometimes mortifying degrees—in women. We are presented with more resistance when we take up space, venture into the unknown, and claim what we deserve. But we are more than capable of doing so. Every person has the right to pursue their own happiness, whatever that may look like, provided that their happiness doesn't cause harm to another.

Don't be afraid to grow, to expand, to think big, and to own the space you're in. You are where you're supposed to be—you being here is proof. Have confidence in that. A silly practice that can help you grow, open up, and expand is to turn on music and dance like a crazy person. Throw your arms and legs around, pretend you're doing some fashionable new modern dance, and take up the space that you have every right to take up.

Y — yin & yang.

> "Let us give thanks for our shadows
> for they are there in the first place
> because of the presence of light."
> —Kamand Kojouri

Reflection:

Yin and yang are counterparts, yet they are perpetually and seamlessly becoming one another—they are forever connected and interdependent, and they are bound together. Night blends into day, day blends into night, and together they make a whole. We need both light and dark for either of the two to make sense, just as we need cold to appreciate warmth and pain to appreciate joy. It is through pain, after all, that we are able to grow and extend our branches closer to the light.

Taoist Yin and Yang philosophy, introduced in the book Tao Te Ching by the Chinese philosopher Lao Tsu (6th c. B.C.), is a fundamental concept in traditional Chinese medicine, which serves as the foundation for how diagnoses are made and what treatments will be employed. Illnesses are not considered something apart from the body but an imbalance of yin or yang. We can use yin and yang philosophy in our lives to realign with our balance. When you're feeling an excess of yang (fast, focused, solid, hot, dry, aggressive; associated with fire, sky, the sun, masculinity, and daytime), you can incorporate more yin (slow, yielding, diffuse, cold, wet, soft, passive; associated with water, earth, the moon, femininity, and night), and vice versa. This process is always flowing, in search of equilibrium, and embraces both parts to find the whole.

L— harmonize.

"Happiness is not a matter of intensity but of balance, order, rhythm and harmony."
—Thomas Merton

"He who lives in harmony with himself lives in harmony with the universe."
—Marcus Aurelius

Reflection:

For there to be harmony, different notes must come together. When those notes find balance and unity and bring out the best in each other, the result is exquisite. Diversity is beautiful. Differences are important. In finding the most pleasing way to combine those different elements and focusing on what is in agreement, we find harmony in our lives and in our world. We are in harmony with ourselves when what we think, feel, say, and do are in agreement; when our actions ring true with our values, and our values are in vibration with our essence of being. We are in harmony with others when we use our similarities to find common ground while recognizing that our differences are what allows us to create an interesting and dynamic song. We are in harmony with the Universe when we see how our existence contributes to the grand composition of everything.

About the Author, Kate Vredevoogd

The evergreen trees and Pacific Ocean of Western Washington painted my childhood with a palette of blues, grays and greens, which, in my twenties, I traded for the dazzling blue sky, crystalline water and green palm leaves of the Mediterranean Coast. After receiving B.A. degrees in Linguistics and Spanish, I hit the road with my dear friend, Miette. We drove across the country, and then I moved to Spain. That adventure gave me the story for my first book *From the Same Quiver: A Confessional Tale of Wanderlust, Friendship and the Pursuit of Self-Identity*, which was my first collaboration with Miette. Wanderlust Words Publications & Blog was created in January 2021, and has become my main via of self-expression and spiritual expansion.

https://www.wanderlustwords.com/

https://www.instagram.com/kateinspain/

About the Artist, Miette Bennich

I was born in Bellingham, Washington, where I lived until graduating from college. After a life-changing cross country road trip with my best friend, a "gap year" on the East coast that never ended, and a few adventures in between, I swapped the mountains and trees I grew up with for the arid steppes and columnar basalt of the Columbia Basin where I live with *mein Schatz*, my children, my garden, and my paints.

https://www.instagram.com/miette_paints/

www.ingramcontent.com/pod-product-compliance
Lightning Source LLC
Chambersburg PA
CBHW061122070526
44583CB00028B/3358